STEM Milestones
Historic Inventions and Discoveries

# GALILEO, JUPITER'S MOONS, AND THE TELESCOPE

Eileen S. Coates

PowerKiDS press
New York

Published in 2019 by The Rosen Publishing Group, Inc.
29 East 21st Street, New York, NY 10010



Editor: Tanya Dellaccio
Book Design: Reann Nye

Photo Credits: Cover, p. 1 SHEILA TERRY/SCIENCE PHOTO LIBRARY/Getty Images; p. 5 https://commons.wikimedia.org/wiki/File:Justus_Sustermans_-_Portrait_of_Galileo_Galilei,_1636.jpg; p. 6 GraphicaArtis/Archive Photos/Getty Images; p. 7 Mansell/The LIFE Picture Collection/Getty Images; p. 9 https://commons.wikimedia.org/wiki/File:A_nun,_traditionally_identified_as_Suor_Maria_Celeste,_daugh_Wellcome_L0031890.jpg; pp. 11 (top), 12,13 (bottom) Science & Society Picture Library/SSPL/Getty Images; pp. 11 (bottom),17 (bottom) Print Collector/Hulton Fine Art Collection/Getty Images; p. 13 (top) Bettmann/Getty Images; p. 14 Universal History Archive/Universal Images Group/Getty Images; p. 15 https://commons.wikimedia.org/wiki/File:The_Galilean_satellites_(the_four_largest_moons_of_Jupiter).tif; p. 17 (top) Hulton Archive/Getty Images;
p. 19 Photo Josse/Leemage/Corbis Historical/Getty Images;
p. 21 ullstein bild Dtl./Getty Images.

Library of Congress Cataloging-in-Publication Data

Names: Coates, Eileen S., author.
Title: Galileo, Jupiter's moons, and the telescope / Eileen S. Coates.
Description: New York : PowerKids Press, [2019] | Series: STEM milestones: historic inventions and discoveries | Includes index.
Identifiers: LCCN 2018031185| ISBN 9781538343579 (library bound) | ISBN 9781538345207 (pbk.) | ISBN 9781538345214 (6 pack)
Subjects: LCSH: Galilei, Galileo, 1564-1642–Juvenile literature. | Astronomers–Italy–Biography–Juvenile literature. | Scientists–Italy–Biography–Juvenile literature. | Telescopes–History–Juvenile literature. | Discoveries in science–Juvenile literature. | Jupiter (Planet)–Satellites–Juvenile literature. | CYAC: Galileo, 1564-1642.
Classification: LCC QB36.G2 C63 2019 | DDC 520/.92 [B] –dc23
LC record available at https://lccn.loc.gov/2018031185

Manufactured in the United States of America

CPSIA Compliance Information: Batch #CWPK19. For Further Information contact Rosen Publishing, New York, New York at 1-800-237-9932

# CONTENTS

# CHANGING THE WORLD

Galileo Galilei was a scientist who lived hundreds of years ago. His inventions and discoveries helped change the way we look at the world. He invented a **telescope** that helped people look far into the sky. With the telescope, they could even see distant planets!

At that time, most people believed that Earth was the center of the **universe** and that everything in the **solar system** moved around it. When Galileo looked through his telescope, he saw things differently. His invention showed that Earth and all the other planets traveled around the sun.

Galileo spent his life discovering new things about Earth and the solar system. His ideas and **theories** helped us learn more about the world and how to study it.

>

# A LOVE FOR MATH

Galileo was born in Pisa, Italy, on February 15, 1564. His father, Vincenzo, was a musician. His mother's name was Giulia. He had five or six brothers and sisters. His family moved to Florence, Italy, when he was young.

### FASCINATING FINDINGS

Galileo was one of the first scientists to use the scientific method. This is a way of observing, measuring, and experimenting on a **hypothesis** to test ideas and theories. His studies in math helped him carry out many of his experiments.

In 1597, Galileo invented a type of compass—a tool for measuring angles. Galileo sold his invention and made quite a bit of money.

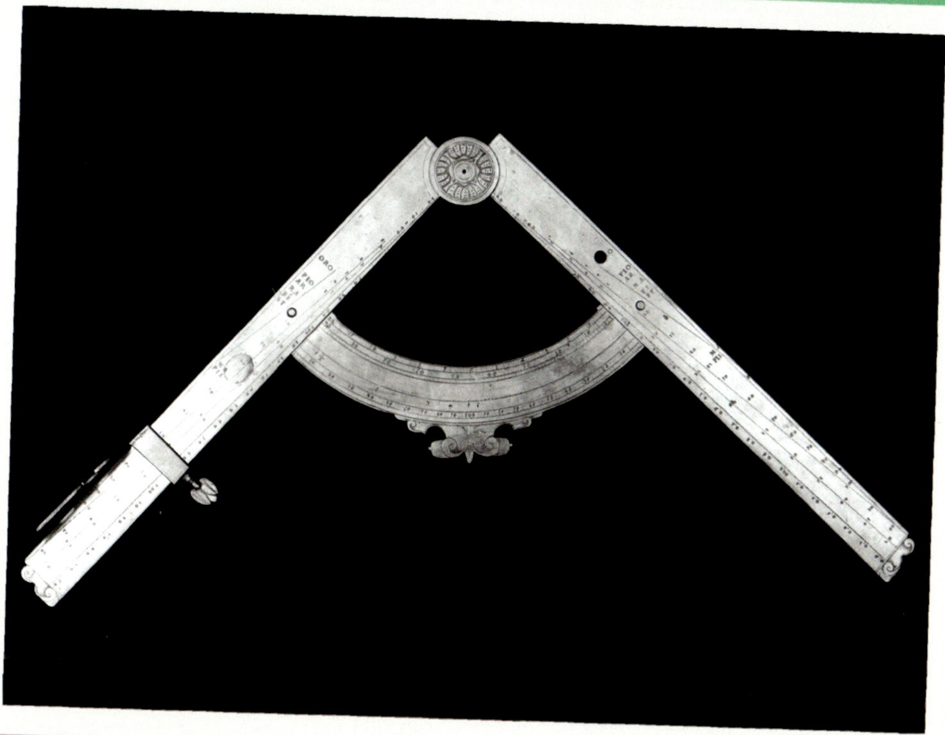

In 1581, Galileo returned to Pisa to study at the University of Pisa. He began studying to become a doctor. However, he soon became more interested in **mathematics** and decided to study that subject. After leaving the university in 1585 without finishing his studies, he began teaching.

# FAMILY FIRST

A few years later, Galileo returned to the University of Pisa and took a job as the head of the mathematics department. Galileo's father died in 1591. A year later, Galileo and his family moved to Padua, Italy. Since Galileo was the oldest son in his family, he took care of his brothers and sisters. He began teaching math and **astronomy** at the University of Padua in 1592.

During Galileo's time in Padua, he had three children with a woman named Marina Gamba. Their first daughter, Virginia, was born in 1600. They later had another daughter, Livia, and a son, Vincenzio.

Both of Galileo's daughters became nuns. His oldest daughter, Virginia, is pictured here. After becoming a nun, she changed her name to Maria Celeste.

>

# WEIGHT AND MOTION

During Galileo's time at both universities, he started doing experiments to study weight and motion. He had a theory that all objects, when dropped, will accelerate, or speed up, at the same rate. The rate doesn't depend on the object's weight. He tested this by dropping things with different weights from the same height.

Galileo used this idea when studying pendulums. A pendulum is a weight hanging from a fixed point so it can swing freely back and forth. He discovered that no matter how high the weight swings, it takes the same amount of time for it to swing from one side to another.

## FASCINATING FINDINGS

Galileo's theory was that no matter the weight of the falling object, **gravity** pulls objects dropped at the same time to the ground at the same rate. U.S. space travelers tested this on the moon in 1971. Since there is no air in space, there's nothing to slow objects falling to the ground. The Apollo 15 commander dropped a hammer and a feather from the same height, and both hit the moon's surface at the same time.

GALILEO'S PENDULUM CLOCK

According to stories, Galileo dropped objects of different weights from the top of the Leaning Tower of Pisa in Pisa, Italy, to test his theory.

# A DIFFERENT VIEW

Galileo began studying telescopes in 1609. Early telescopes were tubes with a piece of curved glass, called a lens, on the inside of each end. The pieces of curved glass refracted, or bent, light as it entered the tube. This magnified faraway objects so people could see them better.

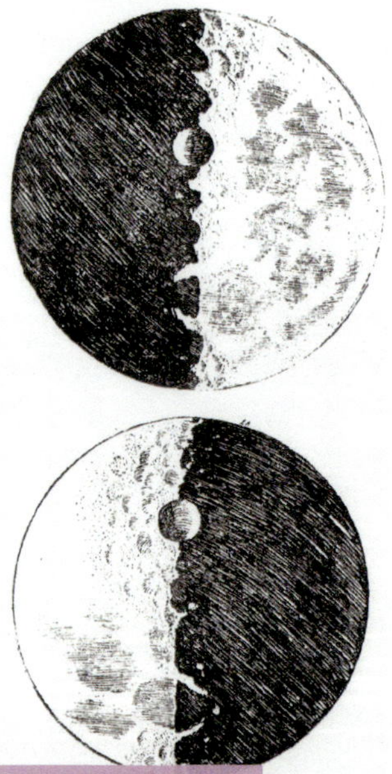

GALILEO'S SKETCHES OF THE MOON

## FASCINATING FINDINGS

Galileo's telescope magnified objects 20 times. He could even see the moon's surface. Scientists at that time believed that the moon's surface was smooth, but Galileo's telescope showed that the surface was uneven with many imperfections.

In 1608, a Dutch eyeglass maker named Hans Lippershey was the first person to apply for a patent, or the official rights to an invention, for a telescope. His telescope could magnify objects three times.

HANS LIPPERSHEY

GALILEO'S TELESCOPE

Even though Galileo didn't invent the first telescope himself, he did have ideas to make it more useful. He used math to figure out how to change the lenses to magnify faraway objects even more. Galileo made the first telescope through which people could see objects in space.

# THE TRUTH IN THE TELESCOPE

Aristotle was a Greek scientist born in 384 BC. He said that all the planets **revolved** around Earth. People believed this for almost 2,000 years. In the 1500s, Polish scientist Nicolaus Copernicus suggested that Earth and the other planets revolved around the sun. Though Copernicus couldn't prove his theory then, Galileo did many years later.

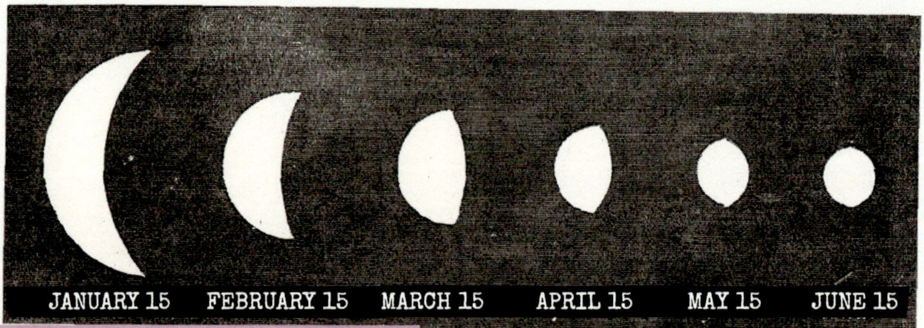


PHASES OF VENUS IN 1859

## FASCINATING FINDINGS

Galileo noticed that Venus looked different as time passed. He figured out that this meant that Venus **orbited** around the sun. The planet looked different because it was traveling farther away from Earth and then coming back again.

Galileo's discovery of some of Jupiter's moons meant that not everything revolved around Earth. Scientists continue to discover new moons, too. As of 2018, Jupiter had 79 known moons!

THE GALILEAN MOONS

In 1610, Galileo, looking through his telescope, saw four moons traveling around Jupiter. He also discovered that the planet Venus goes through phases, which means that the way it looks from Earth changes throughout the year. His findings proved not only that planets didn't revolve around Earth, but that they revolved around the sun.

# THE CHURCH'S WARNING

The Catholic Church was very powerful in Italy during the time Galileo was making his discoveries. The church's leaders firmly supported Aristotle's teachings on the universe and felt that anything that went against them was a crime against the church and its beliefs.

In 1616, the church banned anything suggesting the sun was the center of the universe, including Nicolaus Copernicus's book. It was illegal for people to read or share this information. The church's leaders warned Galileo that his discoveries were incorrect and that he wasn't to speak publicly about his theories about the orbit of planets around the sun.

NICOLAUS COPERNICUS

Nicolaus Copernicus died in 1543. Before his death, he published a book that explained his theory of the sun as the center of the solar system. Below is a drawing of the Copernican system.

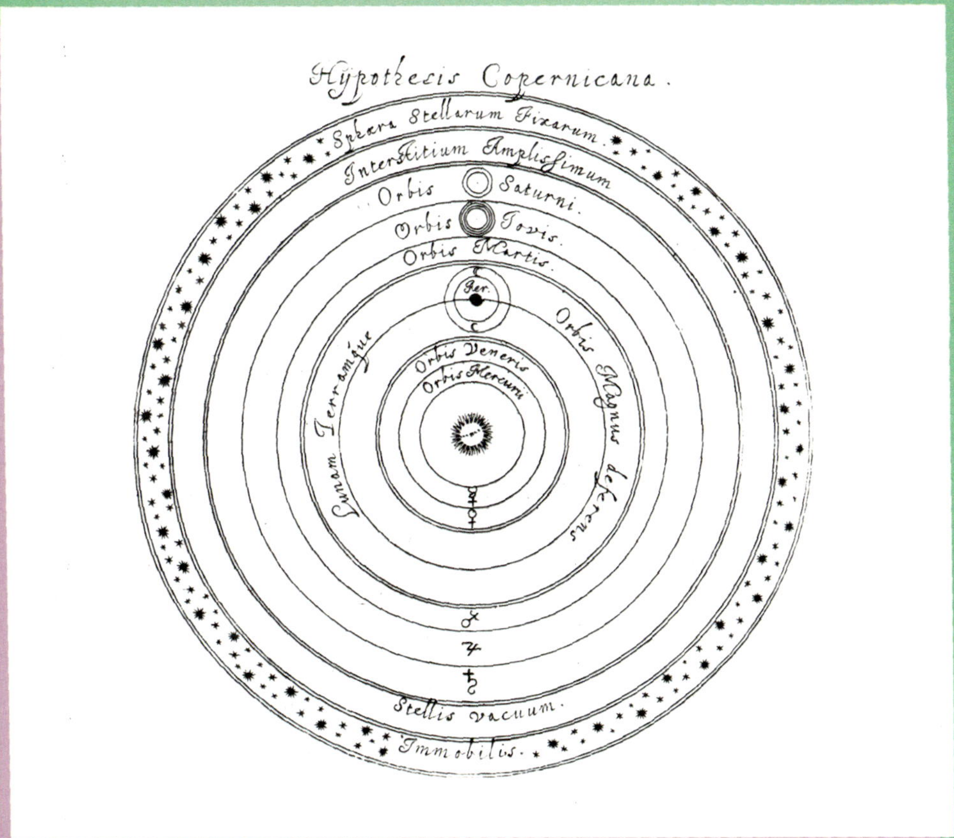

# FACING TRIAL

In 1632, Galileo published a book titled *Dialogue Concerning the Two Chief World Systems*. He wrote of his findings about Earth's orbit and gave **evidence** that the sun was in fact the center of the universe. In 1633, he was called to Rome, Italy, for a **trial**. He was charged with heresy, which is going against the church's teachings and beliefs.

Galileo was Catholic. He argued that he wasn't against the church and that his book just showed the idea of a universe centered on the sun. Still, he was found guilty and sentenced to house arrest, which meant that he wasn't allowed to leave his home for the rest of his life.

Galileo was tried by the Roman Inquisition, a system created by the Catholic Church to try people accused of going against Catholic teachings. Galileo was almost 70 when he was sentenced.

# THE FATHER OF MODERN SCIENCE

Even after his trial, Galileo continued working on his theories. He died in Arcetri, Italy, on January 8, 1642. Galileo's telescope and discoveries in astronomy changed the way people look at the universe.

Though once **controversial**, Galileo's findings helped us understand space and the solar system. In 1989, NASA launched a spacecraft to study Jupiter and its moons. They named the spacecraft the Galileo. Scientists still study Galileo's theories and inventions today. Because of him, we understand more about our place in the stars.

Galileo's discoveries in space have helped us learn more about Earth and where it fits into our solar system. Because of this, he's referred to as the father of modern science!

>

# THE LIFE OF GALILEO GALILEI

**February 15, 1564**
Galileo is born in Pisa, Italy.

**1581**
Galileo begins studying at the University of Pisa.

**1592**
Galileo begins teaching math and astronomy at the University of Padua.

**1600**
Marina Gamba and Galileo have their first child, Virginia.

**1608**
Hans Lippershey patents the first telescope.

**1610**
After creating his new telescope, Galileo sees four of Jupiter's moons.

**1616**
The Catholic Church bans anything suggesting the sun is the center of the universe. Galileo gets a warning.

**1632**
Galileo publishes his book on his theories about the universe and Earth's orbit.

**1633**
Galileo is tried for heresy and sentenced to house arrest for the rest of his life.

**January 8, 1642**
Galileo dies in Arcetri, Italy.

# GLOSSARY

**astronomy:** The study of stars, planets, and other heavenly bodies.

**controversial:** Likely to give rise to disagreement.

**evidence:** Something that shows that something else is true.

**gravity:** The force that pulls objects toward the center of a planet.

**hypothesis:** An idea or theory that hasn't been proven yet.

**mathematics:** The science of numbers and shapes and the relationships between them.

**orbit:** To travel in a circle or oval around something, or the path used to make that trip.

**revolve:** To turn around a center point.

**solar system:** The sun and all the space objects that orbit it, including the planets and their moons.

**telescope:** A tool that makes faraway objects look bigger and closer.

**theory:** An idea or set of ideas to explain facts or events.

**trial:** A meeting in a court in which evidence about crimes is presented.

**universe:** All of space and everything in it.

# INDEX



# WEBSITES

Due to the changing nature of Internet links, PowerKids Press has developed an online list of websites related to the subject of this book. This site is updated regularly. Please use this link to access the list: www.powerkidslinks.com/hiad/telescope